21 SPIRI... VER

SMALL CHANGES THAT BRING RESULTS!

by
Taffi L. Dollar

Harrison House
Tulsa, Oklahoma

TABLE OF CONTENTS

Preface 4

Day 1: Choose What's Best 5

Day 2: Esteeming God 9

Day 3: Trusting Christ First 14

Day 4: Keep Yourself From Idols 18

Day 5: Love Not the World 22

Day 6: Time, Talk, Thought 27

Day 7: Ministering to the Lord..........................31

Day 8: Do Not Fret..36

Day 9: Before All Things 40

Day 10: Our Father...44

Day 11: The High Priest of Our Confession 48

Day 12: Abiding in Him...52

Day 13: Children 57

Day 14: Food and Fasting 61

Day 15: We Are the Lord's.....................................65

Day 16: The Temple..69

Day 17: Christian Busyness 73

Day 18: Hearing God's Voice 77

Day 19: Being God-Conscious 80

Day 20: A New Attitude...85

Day 21: Choices 90

Day 1

CHOOSE WHAT'S BEST

Everything is permissible (allowable and lawful) for me; but not all things are helpful (good for me to do, expedient and profitable when considered with other things). Everything is lawful for me, but I will not become the slave of anything or be brought under its power.

1 Corinthians 6:12 AMP

From time to time it is a wonderful thing to confront ourselves and see where we are in God. Then we can make the changes we need to make so He can continue to take us to places in Him we have never been before and show us things we have never seen before. He can unlock mysteries, give us new strategies to fulfill our callings, and free us from old ways of thinking and doing that have kept us from enjoying our lives in Him.

When you begin to set priorities according to God's Word, you will find you are doing a lot of fine-tuning. As 1 Corinthians 6:12 above says, we have tremendous freedom in Jesus, but we want to make the best choices instead of mediocre or bad choices. And we certainly want to make sure that movies don't have any rule over our lives. The verse also says, "I will not become the slave of anything or be brought under its power." Although I did not feel like I was a slave to these scary movies, and I knew my authority in Jesus over any fear they caused, when the Holy Spirit impressed me to give them up I knew they were a weight I needed to lay aside.

Another example of something being lawful but not expedient is when we adopt the lifestyle and habits of other ministers and Believers. We emulate them because we look up to them, but then we wonder why we don't see the same results in our lives. Even though imitating other strong Christians can bring some good perspectives and habits into our lives, eventually we find out that in order to be where God wants us to be, we have to live our lives the way He wants *us* to live them. It isn't that what other Believers are doing is bad; it is just that what they are doing is not what God wants *us* to be doing.

Other Believers may be able to watch movies about serial killers. It could be God has called them into professions where the information in these movies would give them insight and wisdom. But they were not for me! If I modeled my life after those Believers' lives, my walk with the Lord would be hindered. Therefore, it

Day 2

ESTEEMING GOD

By him were all things created, that are in heaven, and that are in earth, visible and invisible, whether they be thrones, or dominions, or principalities, or powers: all things were created by him, and for him: And he is before all things, and by him all things consist. And he is the head of the body, the church: who is the beginning, the firstborn from the dead; that in all things he might have the preeminence.

Colossians 1:16-18

Do you believe what you just read? If you do, then your life should reflect "the preeminence" of Jesus Christ. He created you. He created the earth and every material thing you enjoy. He redeemed you from sin and gave you His righteousness, peace, and joy in the Holy Ghost. He is the head of the Church and His Body, of which you are a vital member. He holds the universe together, and He will hold your life together if you will let Him!

Colossians 1:16 also says that we were created *for* Him. We are here on Earth for His pleasure and for His purpose. This verse tells me that before I was born, even before He created the heavens and the Earth, don't know His will if we don't talk with Him, and we won't stay in His will if we don't stay in communication with Him.

If we don't set the priorities in our lives, circumstances and people will. And setting priorities begins with esteeming God before anything or anyone else. The Bible talks about how the Macedonian Believers did this even as they were dealing with very hard times.

> **Moreover, brethren, we do you to wit of the grace of God bestowed on the churches of Macedonia;**
>
> **How that in a great trial of affliction the abundance of their joy and their deep poverty abounded unto the riches of their liberality.**
>
> **For to their power, I bear record, yea, and beyond their power they were willing of themselves;**
>
> **Praying us with much intreaty that we would receive the gift, and take upon us the fellowship of the ministering to the saints.**
>
> **And this they did, not as we hoped, but first gave their own selves to the Lord, and unto us by the will of God.**
>
> **2 Corinthians 8:1-5**

The Macedonian Believers were going through a "great trial of affliction" and "deep poverty." Yet, they had an abundance of joy. How did they do that? The answer is found in verse 5, which says that they "first gave their own selves to the Lord." They esteemed Him

SETTING YOUR PRIORITIES TODAY
His mercies are new every morning!

Throughout your day today, keep track of what you think about. Are you giving the Lord your undivided attention whenever possible? Do you consult Him as you make all the little decisions as well as the big decisions? Whether you are a busy professional or a wife and mother going in five directions at the same time, you can train yourself to meditate on God's Word and commune with the Holy Spirit. This is esteeming God in your life.

You cannot fully trust anyone but Christ. You can't trust this world. The news media is frequently biased so you can't trust them. People who don't know or follow the Lord are usually thinking only of themselves and what they want. And how many Believers have turned their backs on God because instead of trusting first in Christ they trusted in some TV preacher who fell? Even other Believers can compromise, get weighed down with hidden sins and cares, and refuse to surrender certain areas of their lives to the Lord. So it is important that your bottom-line trust is in Christ and Christ alone.

To live a life that means something and pleases God, you must choose to trust Him before you get out of bed in the morning and throughout your day. No matter what hard times you face or desperate situations you find yourself in, you choose to trust Him to see you through to victory. You seek first His counsel and let the Holy Spirit and the Word direct your path.

In 1 Timothy 5, Paul talks about how wives and widows should conduct themselves. In verses 11 and 12 he rebukes the young widows who have turned to worldly pursuits instead of putting God first. The language he uses is extremely strong. He says, "Having damnation, because they have cast off their first faith." Damnation is experiencing the opposite of God's love and blessing. In practical, everyday terms, it means that

When you put God first and trust in Him, you won't have to compromise your beliefs or moral standards to have friends, find a mate, or live a valuable and happy life. When you live a godly life you will draw others who also do the same. You will also draw people who may desire to live a godly life. Then, when your life on earth is over, you'll have a sense of peace because you trusted Christ.

SETTING YOUR PRIORITIES TODAY
His mercies are new every morning!

Examine yourself today. Ask the Holy Spirit to reveal any hypocrisy or self-deception, pride, or arrogance, where you really trust more in yourself or someone or something else than you trust in Christ. Decide that in every moment of today and the days to come, Jesus is the first person you will look to for help and comfort. He is your best friend and wisest counselor. When you set this simple priority, to trust Him first, you will find yourself living a life that means something.

relationship or activity that has replaced God by becoming our first priority. That is idolatry.

My husband and I have a wonderful relationship and marriage. I love, respect, and admire him. But he is not my God. If my devotion to him overshadowed or replaced my devotion to God, I would be worshipping a false god. Idolatry is worshipping and being devoted to false gods. The only true God is the God of the Bible, the Father of Jesus Christ.

When you worship someone or something, you make them the first priority and final authority in your life. If watching sports is your idol, then you set your priorities and arrange your life around sports. If God is truly your God, then you set your priorities and arrange your life by His Word and the leading of His Spirit. It's really just that simple.

I've said this before, but it bears repeating. Going to church a couple of times a week is not giving God first priority in your life. You cannot go to church and worship God with a passion, live like the world the rest of the time, and keep yourself from worshipping idols. If you think and speak and live like the world, you will be devoted to the things the world is devoted to. To keep yourself from idols, you must keep your heart and mind from being captured by anything and anyone other than Jesus Christ.

Jesus must always be your *first* love. You can love other people. You can enjoy all kinds of activities. You can even spend time with unbelievers and work in the

When we put God first we will keep ourselves from idols, and everything else will be in order. Our family will be in order, and we won't have to neglect them and compromise our beliefs to be successful. God wants us to keep ourselves from idols because He has the best plan, the best way, and the greatest blessings to give us.

First John 5:20 above says that Jesus came and gave us an understanding of these things "that we may know him that is true, and we are in him that is true." This is a powerful statement! We literally abide and live and operate in Him, who is *true.* Therefore, we can discern the lies of the enemy, the deceptions and distractions of the world, and anything else that would try to draw us away from God and bring us into the bondage of idolatry. Being in Jesus we can live like Jesus, who was *in* the world but not *of* the world, because we have His understanding.

SETTING YOUR PRIORITIES TODAY
His mercies are new every morning!

Be honest with yourself today. Who or what has captured your heart? What do you think about and spend your energy on more than anything else? If there is anything or anyone else who gets more of your attention than Jesus, it's time to back away from it or them. Then acknowledge Jesus in everything you think, say, and do instead of just nodding to Him from time to time when you need help. Keep yourself from idols by being His partner in life.

forever. My children will have eternal life. That's why I tell my children, "You want me to get before God!" They know that if I put God first, spend time with Him, and commune with Him all day, I will have the love, wisdom, patience, and courage to do what is right for them. I will be effective and productive as their mother and love them in the right way.

If I stay away from God and get caught up in my kids' schedules, suddenly I am just a taxi service who's running them here and there, at my wit's end, and no good to anybody. I have no peace. I have no joy. Consequently, I have no wisdom or patience to deal with all the little foxes that are nipping away at me through my children. They are just trying to grow up, and they need me to be strong in God so I can help them sort out their lives according to the Word of God and learn to follow the Spirit for themselves.

The first example our children have is us. If we live our lives with God as our first priority, then it is almost certain that they will too. By putting God first in our lives, we not only have the grace to be good parents but we also help to insure that our kids will walk in that same grace when they are adults and have children of their own. "Train up a child in the way he should go: and when he is old, he will not depart from it" (Proverbs 22:6).

to jealousy and envy, to anger and rage, to strife and war with others because you always want more and are never fulfilled. What's worse, you commit spiritual adultery and act like God's enemy, as Adam did when he sinned against God in the Garden.

Thank God what Jesus did on Calvary is far greater than what Adam did in the Garden of Eden! By God's grace given to us in Jesus Christ, we can overcome the lusts of this world and not fulfill the lusts of our flesh. If God's grace was sufficient for Paul to overcome his thorn in the flesh, His grace can enable us to defeat the lusts of our flesh, the enticements of the world, and love only Him. How do I know this? Because God's Word says in Acts 10:34 that He is no respecter of persons, that He is faithful to perform His Word for anyone who puts their trust in Him and only Him.

There is a lot at stake here! God has placed a destiny in your heart, and the enemy and the world will do anything they can to talk you out of it or take it and use it for evil. The world is not your friend! And if you try to be the world's friend or do things the world's way, you will be robbed of your divine destiny. The only way to avoid this heartbreak is to put God first at all times and in all situations. You must trust Him, His Word, and follow His Spirit over what the world says or does. He is the only one who can take you where you really want to go!

Day 6

TIME, TALK, THOUGHT

Examine yourselves, whether ye be in the faith; prove your own selves....

2 Corinthians 13:5

We are to examine ourselves regularly to make sure we are walking in the faith of God. One of the clearest ways to determine whether or not we are in the faith is to look at our priorities. Is Jesus still our first love? If He is, He will show up in every area of our lives.

There are three ways we can tell what our priorities are: how we spend our time, what we talk about, and what we think about. How do you spend your time? What do you find yourself doing when you are not working or taking care your family? Are you laid up in front of the television all evening long, all day long? Are you at the mall shopping for stuff you don't need? Are you chatting on the Internet or playing video games for hours at a time?

There's nothing wrong with any of these activities as long as your time with the Lord comes first. You have to set the priority of having time with Him. Don't wait to find the time, because it won't happen. The angels are not going to come down, snatch the remote control out

(NKJV) says it best, "Let your speech always be with grace, seasoned with salt, that you may know how you ought to answer each one." We should always be speaking in line with the truth of God's Word, planting seeds of truth with grace into every life we touch. This eliminates gossip! If we are always talking about other people and their business, then we are not walking in the grace and love of God, and He is not our first priority.

The third way we can tell our priorities is what we think about. What do we meditate on when our minds are not occupied with family, work, or ministry? Psalm 1:1-3 says that if we meditate on the Word of God day and night, we will be blessed and successful in every area of our lives. The battle of good and evil is won between our ears. What we think about most is going to determine whether Jesus is Lord, or the devil has his way with us.

In this battle, our only offensive weapon is the sword of the Spirit, which is the Word of God. (See Ephesians 6:12-17.) The Bible tells us to continually renew our minds with God's Word so that whenever we face temptation, persecution, tragedy, or some other attack of the enemy, we will stand strong in faith. When God and His Word are our first priority, we have the faith and wisdom to win every battle we fight.

All three of these things—time, talk, and thought—reveal our priorities, and they are interrelated. How we spend our time affects what we think and what we

Day 7

MINISTERING TO THE LORD

Now there were in the church that was at Antioch certain prophets and teachers; as Barnabas, and Simeon that was called Niger, and Lucius of Cyrene, and Manaen, which had been brought up with Herod the tetrarch, and Saul.

As *they ministered to the Lord,* and fasted, the Holy Ghost said, Separate me Barnabas and Saul for the work whereunto I have called them.

Acts 13:1-2 (italics mine)

The Holy Spirit gives us a picture of the saints at Antioch, and we can see that He spoke clearly to them when they ministered to the Lord. When Jesus is our first priority, we will minister to Him. But what does that mean in practical terms? Is it fasting, as is mentioned in verse 2? Is it praying? Is it doing what He's called us to do?

Recently I began to understand more about what ministering to the Lord really is. I would hear Creflo sing around the house and realize that he was ministering to the Lord in a very simple, easygoing way. Looking at this Scripture, I saw that part of what the saints at Antioch were doing as a fast was to minister to worship becomes a dead ritual and a spiritually dull recital when the saints don't minister to the Lord with their whole hearts. It's great to minister to one another with music, but if we aren't first ministering to the Lord, eventually there will be no ministry to the people either.

> **Hast thou not known? hast thou not heard, that the everlasting God, the LORD, the Creator of the ends of the earth, fainteth not, neither is weary? there is no searching of his understanding.**
>
> **He giveth power to the faint; and to them that have no might he increaseth strength.**
>
> **Even the youths shall faint and be weary, and the young men shall utterly fall:**
>
> **But they that wait upon the LORD shall renew their strength; they shall mount up with wings as eagles; they shall run, and not be weary; and they shall walk, and not faint.**
>
> **Isaiah 40:28-31**

This is one of the most famous and powerful passages of Scripture about the blessings that come from ministering to the Lord. We thank God that He never faints or grows weary, that His understanding of all things—of us especially!—is unlimited, and that He gives us His power and strength to go on when we are mentally, emotionally, and physically drained.

Verse 30 then speaks of a time when even the young people will faint and fall, but verse 31 says that those who "wait upon the Lord" will be strong as eagles, run we receive His strength and wisdom, and He prepares us to run!

SETTING YOUR PRIORITIES TODAY
His mercies are new every morning!

Take the time to minister to the Lord and wait upon Him, and expect Him to speak to you. He's an ever-present help in the time of trouble, always there, longing to commune with you and give you answers and insight. Sing to Him. Let Him know what He means to you. Tell him your whole heart, and then He will tell you His!

really seems impossible! You know how terrifying this world can be. Have You read the news lately?"

In verse 6, God doesn't just tell us not to fret. He also gives us something to do to defeat fear, worry, and anxiety. We are supposed to pray, tell Him what we need, and do it with an attitude of thanksgiving. Now we cannot be thankful if we don't expect something to be thankful for! That's why we make our requests to God in faith, knowing He loves us and already has a solution to our problems.

The next verse talks about the power of our salvation. We can pray to God without being afraid of Him. He revealed His love for us when Jesus died for our sins on the Cross. He breathed His Spirit into us and gave us a new spirit and a new life. Then He sat us right next to Him with Jesus and gave us His authority over all the power of the enemy, over the world, and over our flesh. That's why our hearts and minds can remain in peace!

People who don't make their relationship with God their first priority never get to know Him and the power of their salvation. As a result, they are always fretting and tend to continue to be afraid of Him in a bad way. We are to fear Him in the sense of reverence and awe, but we are never to be afraid of Him because we are His beloved, precious children. And when we see the greatness of our salvation, which is revealed in His

not just setting aside a certain time each
[...] in tongues and make your requests known
[...] hat is very important, but it is only the
[...] because prayer is communication with Him.
[...] n you and you live in Him, so you can talk to
[...] where at any time.

[...] n I spend the day with my family, I talk with them
[...] oy their presence during the whole day. When one
[...] children wants to talk to me about something, I
[...] say, "Not now. It is not our family time." And the
[...] holds true for prayer. I just enjoy God's presence and
[...] e a running conversation with Him throughout my day.

There have been many times when God has stopped
[...] e in my tracks and cautioned me when I was about to
[...] o something that I thought was a good idea. To my
natural mind, everything looked fine, but He knew
something I didn't know. Later, I would see why He
had stopped me. If He had not been before all things in
my life at that moment, keeping me in an attitude of
prayer to hear Him, I would have made a big mistake.

Prayer is also not a formal, religious thing. You don't
have to talk to God in *King James'* English, saying, "I
thank Thee, O Lord, for the bounty that Thou hast
given." He knows how you talk! He hears you talk to your
family and friends. He knows how you talk to yourself! In
fact, He knows more about you than you do. So you best
just drop all the religious jargon and be real with Him.

Then comes the doing. Paul says, "You've learned a
lot of godly things from me. You've learned by watching
my example, by hearing me preach and teach God's
Word, and by spending time with me. So now, go out
and do these things yourself." You can't just hear
something, know about it, and succeed. You must also
do it, appropriate it, and make it a part of your life.

SETTING YOUR PRIORITIES TODAY
His mercies are new every morning!

On one sheet of paper make a list of everything that
makes you fretful, worried, afraid, anxious, tense, or
nervous. Then on another sheet of paper make a list of
what is true, honest, just, pure, lovely, of a good report,
virtuous, or praiseworthy in your life that cancels out
what you put on your "fret list." The assurance of your
salvation is that it is so great, so powerful, that nothing
can stand against it. The Word of God and the Holy
Spirit in you can make your fret list melt away and
disappear forever!

There are lots of prayer groups today, and intercessory prayer has become a big thing in the church. This is good because it reveals the priority and importance of prayer, but it can be detrimental to living a life of prayer. Some Believers go to prayer meetings; passionately pray long, Word-filled prayers; then never pray until the next prayer meeting. Then they wonder why their lives are falling apart. It is because Jesus really doesn't come before anything else in their lives, so they are talking to Him only when they are with other Believers.

We need to make certain that our lifestyle reflects what we say we believe. If Jesus is before all things in our lives, then we will be in an attitude of prayer throughout our day, always communing with Him. The world will see the difference He makes because He will hold our lives together when the world around us is falling apart.

SETTING YOUR PRIORITIES TODAY
His mercies are new every morning!

Today you cannot hold your life together! Only Jesus can do that, which is why you must put Him before all things. If you haven't already done it, establish a private time of prayer each day. Then continue to talk with Him and enjoy His presence for the rest of your day. Your life will become richer and fuller if you determine in your heart to do what the Word of God commands you to do in 1 Thessalonians 5:17, "Pray without ceasing." That means, talk to Jesus now and always!

segments of our life. He's a part of everything we do. On the golf course, at work, and at home, He's there and we talk to Him.

I've just painted a really beautiful picture of fatherhood, but we see very few natural fathers who come close to that picture. Even in the church, many fathers today put their profession before anything else, and their families suffer from their neglect and lack of affection. Some fathers run out on their children through crime and prison, drugs, alcohol, or women other than their wives. Some just leave. Today we have fathers who molest their children or someone else's children. We hear about fathers who murder their families and then take their own lives. Good fathers are hard to find today.

The reason we see this is because a natural father cannot be what he was created to be without making it a priority to know *the Father*.

And mothers are not exempt! Women in society are saying things and doing things I never would have thought of as a young girl growing up. Today they can be just as violent, abusive, and destructive as any man ever was. That's why motherhood has also taken a big hit. Mothers are aborting their babies before they are born and murdering them after they are born. Why? They do not know the Father who created them. If they did, they would be so filled with His love that they could never hurt their children. (See 1 John 4:7-8.)

love is so great that He told me the truth about myself so that I would grow in the integrity of my heart.

Your heavenly Father will reveal your heart to you. He will show you your *self*—the good, the bad, and the ugly—and who He created you to be. I can't tell you these things. In fact, it blesses me when people give their testimonies because I will observe someone and think something about them that isn't true or real at all! When I hear their story I see that I had no idea who they were or what God had brought them through.

Only your Father knows who you really are, why you received the gifts and talents you have, and how you can live your life to the fullest. Your brothers and sisters in Christ can help you discover these things, but only an intimate relationship with Him will make you truly happy and fulfilled.

SETTING YOUR PRIORITIES TODAY
His mercies are new every morning!

Take a good look at your relationship with your earthly father, and then read these Scriptures about your heavenly Father: Matthew 6:8, John 10:27-30 and 14:9, Romans 8:15, 1 Corinthians 8:6, Ephesians 1:17, Hebrews 12:9, and James 1:17. It is also helpful to read through the New Testament and see how many times the Father is mentioned by Jesus and the apostles. Most of us love and cherish our natural fathers, but our Father in Heaven is amazing!

It's not so hard to hold fast to my confession of faith in Jesus when I consider what He has done and continues to do for me. It blows my mind when I try to fathom His love. I can miss the mark yesterday and today I've got a new day! He's not thinking about what I did yesterday, that I didn't do what I should have done or should have known better than to get myself into something. That's why I say at the end of each chapter, "His mercies are new every morning!" (See Lamentations 3:22-23.) Every day I can wake up and know He has forgiven me and my life is fresh and new. I have another chance to get it right.

Jesus is our Lord and Savior and King, and He is also our High Priest. We do not have some high priest who cannot understand and sympathize with our weaknesses and infirmities. We have Jesus, who was tempted and tried and tested in every way that we are—but didn't sin. That makes Him the perfect example to follow. Even though He is perfect, He is also compassionate.

Let us then fearlessly and confidently and boldly draw near to the throne of grace (the throne of God's unmerited favor to us sinners), that we may receive mercy [for our failures] and find grace to help in good time for every need [appropriate help and well-timed help, coming just when we need it].

Hebrews 4:16 AMP

When we are mindful of how merciful God is, and how He is so moved by the things that we go through, we can also remember that He wants to bear our burdens. We

What did we say after that? What was our confession of faith? "God is handling it. It's going to be okay." And I tell you, it was over before we knew it! His was well-timed help—just when we needed it. There's nothing too hard for the High Priest of our confession!

Somebody said once that mankind's extremities are God's opportunities. When it seems hopeless and you are ready to lock your door and never answer the phone again because everyone you owe is after you, when you are backed into a corner because your boss wants you to do something "slightly illegal," when you feel trapped in an unhappy marriage and your kids are embarrassing you—that's the opportunity to go to the High Priest of your confession and receive some mercy and grace! He will understand, He will forgive, He will cleanse you of all unrighteousness and shame, and He will give you the answers you need to overcome.

SETTING YOUR PRIORITIES TODAY
His mercies are new every morning!

Are you facing an overwhelming situation today? In 1 Peter 5:7 the Holy Spirit commands you to cast every care on Him. He says, "Throw it at Me! Roll it over on Me." He wants to relieve you and free you of all worry and fear. You have a High Priest who will take your burdens and give you answers—without condemnation or anger. He understands and has only His mercy and grace for you. Go boldly into His throne room to give Him your troubles and receive what you need from Him right now.

please some other human. That's when the Father prunes you with His Word.

> **Now ye are clean through the word which I have spoken unto you.**
>
> **John 15:3**

The Word of God is a priority because Jesus is the Living Word. God speaks directly and personally to us in the Bible, and when He has an issue with us the Holy Spirit brings the Word to our remembrance. He prunes and cuts away dead and renegade things in our lives with His Word, which cleans us and frees us so that we can bear more fruit for Him.

> **Abide in me, and I in you. As the branch cannot bear fruit of itself, except it abide in the vine; no more can ye, except ye abide in me.**
>
> **I am the vine, ye are the branches: He that abideth in me, and I in him, the same bringeth forth much fruit: for without me ye can do nothing.**
>
> **If ye abide in me, and my words abide in you, ye shall ask what ye will, and it shall be done unto you.**
>
> **John 15:4-5,7**

We are created and commanded to be fruitful and multiply, but God has set things up so that we cannot bear fruit unless we are connected to Him, abiding in Him. We must live and move and have our being in Him. (See Acts 17:28.) Then His love and life and cars and have a fight. By the time we get to work we are in strife with our coworkers, and we take absolutely no joy in what we do. We are bound up and can bear no fruit. Abiding in the Word is a much better way to live!

Abiding in Jesus brings peace, serenity, tranquility, joy, and a new sense of purpose. Praying and abiding in Him also causes us to make some changes in how we govern ourselves. It enables us to shake off offenses and forgive quickly. Traffic jams are simply more time spent with the Father! We can trust Him that we will bear the fruit we are supposed to bear that day.

If we abide in Jesus all week, church becomes much more exciting! We all bring what we have learned and experienced with God into the fellowship of other Believers. We are joining together as brothers and sisters, His children, with fully-charged spirits. Somebody has a song. Another has a testimony. One of the saints gives a word of prophecy, and we are all plugged into the Father's heart! Praise and worship is vibrant and alive, and it seems that our pastor preaches the best message we have ever heard. The Word of God pierces our hearts and transforms us. We are forever changed, and we leave the church freshly anointed to bear even more fruit for our Father.

Everything in our lives is charged with the life and love of God when we abide in Him.

Day 13

Children

Samuel ministered before the LORD, being a child, girded with a linen ephod.

1 Samuel 2:18

Even a little child can be used greatly by the Lord when they learn early to love Him and minister to Him. I am thrilled to see the youth and children in our church on fire for the Lord. It not only blesses me, but seeing them put Him first at such an early age puts me under conviction! I had to learn this later in life, and it is so wonderful that they are learning it as children and teens.

You can read the whole story of how Samuel was born and raised in 1 Samuel, chapters 1 and 2. He was a very young boy when his parents took him to Eli the priest to serve the Lord. God had put the desire in Hannah to have a son, and for years she was barren. She continued to pray and seek the Lord to have a son, and she promised to dedicate him to the Lord. That meant that from the moment he was born, she would teach him that God was to be first place in his life.

It is so important to dedicate our children to God and train them to love and serve Him before anyone or was growing up, it wasn't like today. We can read the Bible, hear the Word from many different ministers on television, go to church to be fed the Word, and share with one another to get revelation. But none of that existed in Samuel's world. The Word was "precious," or scarce, and as a result there was no open vision. No one was seeing in the Spirit or hearing from God.

> **Samuel did not yet know the LORD, neither was the word of the LORD yet revealed unto him.**
>
> **1 Samuel 3:7**

Even though Samuel did not yet know the Lord or the Word, he ministered to the Lord under Eli's care, and in chapter 3 we have the story of Eli teaching Samuel to recognize the voice of the Lord. One night in bed Samuel was awakened by somebody calling his name. He called back, "Eli, are you calling me?"

Eli said, "No, it's not me." This happened two times, and on the third time Eli said, "There's something going on with this kid, and I believe it's the Lord." He told Samuel, "If you hear the voice again, say, 'Speak to me, Lord, for I'm Your servant and I hear You.' I believe God is trying to talk to you."

When God spoke to Samuel the third time, he answered as Eli had instructed him. God then gave Samuel his first word of prophecy, and from that time on the Bible says, "And Samuel grew, and the LORD was with him, and did let none of his words fall to the

Day 14

Food and Fasting

Now the Spirit speaketh expressly, that in the latter times some shall depart from the faith, ...

Forbidding to marry, and commanding to abstain from meats, which God hath created to be received with thanksgiving of them which believe and know the truth.

1 Timothy 4:1,3

We are in the latter times, and if there was ever a time to seek God it is now! Who would have thought that we would turn on our televisions to see what we see and hear what we hear today. In brilliant color and high definition we can view violence and crime, all kinds of family dysfunctions, sexual and immoral acts—and that's just the news! But Paul is telling Timothy that one of the big *spiritual* issues in the church would be "abstaining from meats, which God hath created to be received with thanksgiving."

Paul said that Christians are to be thankful for and enjoy all the good food God created, but we cannot let food become our first priority. This is hard because not only does it taste good, our society revolves around food. Fast-food restaurants are on every corner. There is constant advertising in every kind of media, and every time we

Paul goes on to tell Timothy,

Refuse profane and old wives' fables, and exercise thyself rather unto godliness.

For bodily exercise profiteth little: but godliness is profitable unto all things, having promise of the life that now is, and of that which is to come.

1 Timothy 4:7-8

Now don't use verse 8 as an excuse not to exercise! It does profit you and will keep your temple fit for the Lord's use. What the Holy Spirit is saying is that godliness is the main thing we should pursue. Godliness is the priority because you can't live a godly life apart from God. To be like Him you have to spend time with Him and get to know Him in His Word. Godly fasting means putting down the desires of our flesh and seeking only the Lord.

I want to live a godly life and not just be saved. My life is more powerful and has more impact if I practice godliness rather than going around telling people I am a Christian. The title means nothing without the fruit, and the fruit doesn't come without abiding in Jesus. (See John 15:1-8.) The purpose of fasting is to bring us closer to Him and put food—or whatever else we might be fasting from—in its proper place and perspective.

Fasting from food comes from a personal conviction from the Holy Spirit that *we* need to change how we see food and how we use food. We cannot make a doctrine out of it and look down our noses at other

Day 15

WE ARE THE LORD'S

Whether we live, we live unto the Lord; and whether we die, we die unto the Lord: whether we live therefore, or die, we are the Lord's.

Romans 14:8

You are the Lord's treasured possession, and He wants your life to be blessed and fruitful. But He doesn't just snap His fingers and it's done. You have to do your part, too. You must learn who you are in Him, obey Him, and bring your flesh under submission to your spirit. To live a life of balance, a life of temperance that's controlled by the Holy Ghost, you must discipline your body. This is the real victory of your life in Jesus Christ.

Although Romans 14 talks a lot about food, the Holy Spirit is really talking about each Believer's unique walk with the Lord. Each one of us belongs to Him. If all Believers lived just for Him, He wouldn't have had to write this passage of Scripture! But unfortunately, we too often judge and criticize one another when it is none of our business. I know when I find myself doing this, it means I'm looking at the faults and weaknesses of others so I don't have to deal with my own!

"Sweep around your own front porch." And Jesus told us to get the telephone pole out of our own eye. Then we can help get the speck out of another person's eye. (See Luke 6:41-42.) This is a principle of the Kingdom because every Believer answers personally to the Lord. He is their master and they are His servant. We are not their master!

Sometimes we get wrapped up in someone else's problems because we're afraid of facing our own. But verse 4 says that the Lord will support us and make us stand tall and strong. He will sustain us as we deal with the issues and face the challenges of our lives. His grace is sufficient for every situation. There's grace to abide in and obey the Word. There's grace to walk in the Spirit. And there's grace to do what the Lord leads us to do by not judging the faults of others and dealing with our own!

Each of us belongs to the Lord, and His path for you is different from His path for me. I cannot judge my life by yours and you cannot judge your life by mine. We must each judge our lives by the Word and how the Spirit is leading us. If we all kept this priority in our lives, we could probably wipe out all strife in the Body of Christ! So continue to walk with Jesus, knowing He is not only your Master, He is every Believer's Master, too. You are the Lord's—and so are they!

Day 16

THE TEMPLE

I keep under my body, and bring it into subjection: lest that by any means, when I have preached to others, I myself should be a castaway.

1 Corinthians 9:27

In *The Amplified Bible,* this verse reads, "But [like a boxer] I buffet my body [handle it roughly, discipline it by hardships] and subdue it, for fear that after proclaiming to others the Gospel and things pertaining to it, I myself should become unfit [not stand the test, be unapproved and rejected as a counterfeit]." Paul says that he disciplines his body with a godly fear that he should meet the Bible standard of spirituality he has preached to others.

What does this say about fasting? When we honestly seek God through fasting and prayer, we push the flesh aside, deny our appetite's control, and allow our spirit man to develop and to be strengthened. The priority of fasting is to recapture our hunger and rekindle our fire for God. It says to Him, "I am willing to give up anything in order to be in Your presence and do Your will."

Colossians 1:17 says that Jesus is before all things, and when we fast we enforce that in our lives. Whatever

For a long time I watched Creflo take all these vitamins, jumping up in the morning, praising God as he drank his nutrition drink, and it just got on my nerves! We would go out of town and he had this backpack of supplements, and at home he was messing up my beautifully decorated kitchen with all his bottles on the counter. But I began to see the importance of what he was doing when God began to show me that my body was His temple, and I needed to take care of it so I could effectively do His will.

I wish I had learned this before I got pregnant! I just ate everything that wasn't nailed down. No temperance. No wisdom on how to care for God's temple. Then, after having the baby, I was fifty or sixty pounds overweight and all out of shape. I had to work so hard to get back to a normal weight and feel good again. Fasting helped me understand the importance of a healthy body. It gave me a godly reverence for it because the Lord lives in my body. I'm His home, and I want Him to be able to move freely in me and through me.

As a minister, I do not want to hinder the work of the Lord by a body that's out of shape, and I don't want to die early and not fulfill my days because I let my flesh have its way! I want to be a vessel of honor for the Lord's use and a great example to those I teach. So I keep my body under submission to the Word and

Day 17

CHRISTIAN BUSYNESS

Unto the angel of the church of Ephesus write; These things saith he that holdeth the seven stars in his right hand, who walketh in the midst of the seven golden candlesticks;

I know thy works, and thy labour, and thy patience, and how thou canst not bear them which are evil: and thou hast tried them which say they are apostles, and are not, and hast found them liars:

And hast borne, and hast patience, and for my name's sake hast laboured, and hast not fainted.

Nevertheless I have somewhat against thee, because thou hast left thy first love.

Revelation 2:1-4

In this passage of Scripture we find out that Jesus is always walking in our midst. He knows what we are doing and what keeps us busy. So many of us wear a Christian medal of honor that says, "I'm so busy for the Lord." We get so busy for Him that we lose sight of Him! He's right in our midst and we aren't seeing Him or hearing Him. Then we wonder why things go wrong. We scratch our heads, saying, "What are You doing, Lord?"

At that point, usually in a crisis, He's got our full attention and says, "You've lost your first love." He's

> And another also said, Lord, I will follow thee; but let me first go bid them farewell, which are at home at my house.
>
> And Jesus said unto him, No man, having put his hand to the plough, and looking back, is fit for the kingdom of God.

> Luke 9:59-62

Jesus wasn't being insensitive or cruel. He was simply pointing out that following Him means surrendering your whole life to Him. He becomes your whole life. We have to be willing to pay the price to live the life He wants us to live and do His will. Following Him will cost us some things along the way, but in the end the rewards far outweigh what we gave up.

Then there is money! How busy are you just making money? Remember the rich, young ruler? He proudly declared that he had lived a nearly perfect life and was ready to follow Jesus when Jesus said,

> If thou wilt be perfect, go and sell that thou hast, and give to the poor, and thou shalt have treasure in heaven: and come and follow me.
>
> But when the young man heard that saying, he went away sorrowful: for he had great possessions.
>
> Then said Jesus unto his disciples, Verily I say unto you, That a rich man shall hardly enter into the kingdom of heaven.
>
> And again I say unto you, It is easier for a camel to go through the eye of a needle, than for a rich man to enter into the kingdom of God.

> Matthew 19:21-24

Day 18

Hearing God's Voice

He that hath an ear, let him hear what the Spirit saith....
Revelation 2:7

You were created to hear physically and spiritually. Don't be a Christian who is content with not hearing from God, because it grieves Him. He is a Father who desires intimacy with His children. He wants to know you, and He wants you to know Him.

As a mother, if I had children who couldn't hear my voice, that would bother me because they are flesh of my flesh. There is a bond and a desire for relationship that can be achieved only by fellowship and communication one with another, me hearing them and them hearing me. Believe me, I would find other ways of communicating with them like sign language, reading lips, and using the sense of touch.

It would be even more grievous to me if my children were able to hear my voice but refused to take the time to listen to me. It would be a nightmare to talk to children who continually turned away and gave their attention to someone or something else, especially if I was trying to warn them of impending danger, or tell them how to and minds. We have to understand that we are not holy because of what we say or do. We are holy because of the blood of Jesus. That's how God sees us, and we need to see ourselves that way. Then we will speak and act holy because it is who we are. We won't think it strange that our Father would talk to us simply because we are His kids!

If you saw me with my kids and observed that I never spoke to them, you would probably assume I wasn't their mother. But I am their mother and I talk with them all the time. That's the way your Father wants to talk with you!

SETTING YOUR PRIORITIES TODAY
His mercies are new every morning!

When was the last time you had a heart-to-heart talk with your Father? Have you felt nasty and unworthy to talk with Him? Today, take some time to allow the Holy Spirit to show you that He wants to speak to you no matter what condition you think you are in, or really are in. Open your heart and mind to receive whatever He wants to give you: revelation, wisdom, instruction, a correction, or a shot of encouragement. Sometimes all we need is a simple revelation that He wants to talk to us to open our ears and hear all He has to say. Those are the moments that change our lives!

Jesus then says, "Take therefore no thought for the morrow: for the morrow shall take thought for the things of itself" (Matthew 6:34). This is one of the keys to thinking like God, speaking like God, and acting like God. Don't worry about tomorrow! You can consider your options prayerfully and get the direction of the Holy Spirit on paying your bills, but don't worry and wring your hands about how the bills are going to get paid. You seek God first, and God will take care of you.

We have to trust our Father. We've got to get rid of that mindset that says, "I've got to take care of myself because that's what I've always done and no one else is going to do it if I don't." No, that mindset died when we were born again and became children of the Most High God. We are no longer our own little gods because we belong to Him. And when our lives are fully yielded to His will and we seek Him before all else—not worrying—then everything we need in life will be added to us.

To be God-conscious, or God-inside-minded, takes some effort. Nothing just changes by itself, and our minds are no different. To live as a God-conscious person instead of a self-conscious person requires some study and meditation on our part, and then His Word and the Holy Spirit transform us. This is how we learn to think like He thinks and do things the way He does them. Jesus was our perfect example. He demonstrated

We are not meant to always struggle, barely getting by, living from paycheck to paycheck, sick and afraid of dying, about to lose our minds with worry, our kids driving us crazy, and our jobs draining us of every ounce of strength. That's the way world lives, and that's the way Christians live when they do not renew their minds with God's Word and become God-conscious.

I see two extremes in the Body of Christ: those who believe God should do everything and those who believe they should do everything. The truth is in the middle, and we get to the middle by being God-conscious, by knowing that He's our Father and we are His children, and we are in this together. We do our part and He does His. It's a relationship that we develop by renewing our minds with God's Word and learning to think like He thinks.

When we were born again and became new creatures, old things passed away and everything became new—in our spirits. (2 Corinthians 5:17.) Now our souls have to catch the revelation of that and begin to live in it. The Word of God and the Spirit of God bring that revelation from our heads (as we renew our minds) to our hearts (where we believe) and then we are transformed. We are God-conscious.

Believers who renew their minds live like Jesus, not worrying about tomorrow, just following the Spirit and abiding in the Word of God. Being God-conscious,

A New Attitude

Consequently, from now on we estimate and regard no one from a [purely] human point of view [in terms of natural standards of value]. [No] even though we once did estimate Christ from a human viewpoint and as a man, yet now [we have such knowledge of Him that] we know Him no longer [in terms of the flesh].

Therefore if any person is [ingrafted] in Christ (the Messiah) he is a new creation (a new creature altogether); the old [previous moral and spiritual condition] has passed away. Behold, the fresh and new has come!

2 Corinthians 5:16-17 AMP

These verses describe the most important and radical change a human being can undergo. Receiving Jesus Christ as your Lord and Savior should cause an absolute revolution in the way you think, how you talk to others, and the way you conduct yourself. Getting saved is not just a passport to heaven; it is a complete transformation of your character and behavior.

As the song says, you *have a new attitude!*

Unfortunately, when God saved us He did not save us from our old attitude. That's what we have to change. This reminds me of when I got married. I whether we are instantly and completely delivered or we are set free through a process, all Believers have to make the choice to get a new attitude, a Jesus attitude.

You have to do this for the Lord, not to look good in front of your brothers and sisters or impress the boss at work. You can't even change your attitude because I tell you to do it. You have to do it because you know it is the right thing to do, that it is the right thing for you. Third John 2 says that you will prosper to the degree that your soul prospers, and your soul is not prospering if you have an ugly, ungodly attitude!

The old, unregenerate you had an attitude that was selfish and self-centered, negative and fearful. Now you are new on the inside. Your spirit has a new attitude that is loving, giving, positive, loves to serve others, and is filled with faith in a Father God who can do anything. This is what you want to bring from the inside to the outside, from your inward man to your outward man. You do this by doing what Joshua and Caleb did when they went into the Promised Land to spy it out. (See Numbers 13 and 14.) They looked at the situation and maintained a godly attitude by believing God's Word over anything else they saw or experienced. They saw the giants and the great cities, but God had said that the land was theirs. They chose to believe Him.

When you choose to believe and live according to God's Word instead of your carnal reasoning and

Setting Your Priorities Today
His mercies are new every morning!

Make a list of the things that bother you, and you will probably find the attitudes you need to change! Keep in mind that you will be changed only by lining up your thoughts with the Word of God. Change what you believe, and you change your attitude.

For example, the world says the body is the priority. Give it whatever it wants. If it wants to have a milkshake or play tennis or have sex, just do it! The world thinks it is silly to present your body to God as a living sacrifice, but they don't understand the kind of life "living" means. We are alive to God! We have His life in us, and we give that life back to Him. So we choose from moment to moment whether we will live our lives for God or live our lives for ourselves.

The key to making the decision to present ourselves to God instead of serving our flesh is found in the word, "transform." It comes from the Greek word *metamorphoo*, which is where we get the English word, "metamorphosis." Someone or something that goes through a metamorphosis goes through a complete, inside-and-out change in character, condition, appearance, or structure. This is why the word is translated "transform." It means a total change.

In Romans 12:2, it says that we are transformed by the "renewing of [the] mind." This means a complete renovation of our thinking, which we have talked about in this book. When our minds are renewed, we are God-conscious and can make choices in line with His will. We can prove His will by choosing to do things His way and watching the blessed results of that.

It isn't an accident that the butterfly is a great symbol of the Christian life. Before we are saved we exploits for the Kingdom of God. You will lead a fulfilling life, and you will do it all with joy!

SETTING YOUR PRIORITIES TODAY
His mercies are new every morning!

Today I want to give you a declaration to pray over yourself when you need a reminder of who you are in Jesus Christ, and how He is the most important One in your life. Think about what you're saying. Listen to what you're saying. Don't just go through the motions. Allow these words to take root in your mind and capture your heart.

Father, thank You for saving me, healing me, setting me free, and loving me as Your precious child. You are my Father, and You are the Father of spirits, so I am a spirit. Thank You that today I am spiritually alive to You, I live in a body and my soul is renewed and transformed by Your Word. I love Your Word and meditate on it always. I study Your Word and achieve great success in every area of my life. Thank You, Father, that Your Holy Spirit teaches me, comforts me, and guides me with Your truth. He gives direction to my spirit and illumination to my mind. He leads me in the way that I should go in all the affairs of life. In Jesus Christ, Your love is perfected in me and I have an unction from the Holy One, who lives in me. My life today is joy unspeakable and full of glory because I choose to love You and serve You first! In the mighty name of Jesus I pray. Amen.

About the Author

Taffi L. Dollar is a world-renowned author, teacher, and conference speaker who demonstrates God's love to others. As the wife of Dr. Creflo A. Dollar, she co-pastors World Changers Church International (WCCI) and World Changers Church-New York.

A minister of the Gospel, Taffi has a global influence in both ministry and music. She serves as the CEO of Arrow Records, a cutting-edge Christian recording company.

Taffi's commitment to helping others is evident through her lifestyle of service. She founded the Women's Ministry at WCCI to promote unity and sisterhood. In addition, Taffi founded the World Changers Christian Academy Independent Study Program (ISP), an alternative to traditional home schooling. Taffi also serves as an active mentor and sponsor of the Service to Education program at Toney Elementary School in Decatur, Georgia, where she plays an instrumental role in helping students to excel in reading.

With a bachelor's degree in mental health and human services, Taffi has a heart for restoring family relationships. Above all her accomplishments, she considers supporting her husband in ministry and raising godly children her primary purpose. As a mother of five, she firmly believes that the best way to raise successful children is to be an active role model in demonstrating the love of God.

To contact Taffi L. Dollar please write to:

Creflo Dollar Ministries
P.O. Box 490124 • College Park, GA 30349
Tel: 866-477-7683 • **www.creflodollarminstries.com**